M000073377

2021

NEW MOON RITUALS *for* ENTREPRENEURS

Leslie Tagorda

New Moon Rituals for Entrepreneurs / Leslie Tagorda

ISBN 978-1-953449-15-3

MAHALO NUI LOA

. . . .

There are so many beautiful souls to thank for helping me bring this tiny book into the world.

Bevin, my astrology bestie that, back in 2013, helped me create my first BlissKit New Moon Ritual deck, when I was an astrology newbie.

David, my husband, a logical engineer, who always supported my spiritual ways.

Rocket, my teacher and son, who pushes me to be a kinder, more patient soul.

Hello Seven team and community, who have over the last 2 years, pushed and supported me to invest in myself and take risks in my business that have helped me grow exponentially.

The members and listeners of The Savvy Luminary podcast and Facebook community, who have shared their business journeys, for whom I love creating content.

To my vast customers and family from around the globe, who love and believe in me.

And lastly, to Jeff, my right hand person, by my side in my business for the last 10 years, traveling with me and growing with me, always being there when I need any little thing. This book would not be possible without his help.

ALOHA

This book is for you, mystical, powerful, spiritual entrepreneur.

You don't have to know the ins and outs of astro-techie lingo, but if you do, this will serve you too.

All you need is the desire to work with the cosmic cycles and the power cultivated between the dance of the Sun, Moon, and Mother Earth.

If you are called to work with this powerful force, welcome, this book is for you, to deepen your inner wisdom, you already carry with you in your bones, to work with the moon to grow your soilless garden, your business.

NEW MOONS ARE MY JAM

· ·

I've been doing New Moon rituals since 2012. Back then, my life felt pretty hopeless. I was close to 40, single, not super thrilled with my business and feeling stuck!

As I began my regular monthly practice of setting intentions through beautiful rituals, my life began to blossom. Within the span of 3 years I got married, had a child, and reinvented my business combining my expertise as a brand designer and passion in astrology in a unique way in business and brand astrology.

8 years later, I continue to harness the New Moon energy in my personal life, along with my young son, and in group settings with my business.

In this book, my desire is to show you how to hold space and create your own monthly intentions, directed by the stars, to help all your efforts grow.

I want to share this practical magic with you.

Why New Moons?
The New Moon is a perfect time for you to set intentions because the Moon's energy is primed to expand. These practical rituals are designed to harness the New Moon's energy, and made more potent, using the specific power of the zodiac sign in which the Moon becomes new. As you complete each monthly ritual, you will touch on all aspects of your life, planting the seeds for your best self yet, whether you have dreams of love, creativity, inner peace or abundance.

WHAT ARE NEW MOON INTENTIONS?

New Moons are a time to plant your seeds of intention. Your activation is specific and unique to you and your energies. There is no right or wrong way to do your ritual.

◇ **Go big** Imagine the feeling, the belief you have when you have this intention. Are your dreams big enough?
◇ **Let go** Release the how, how-tos, and strategies to get there. There is time for that later, don't let details get in the way of your big dream.
◇ **Write it down** Keep a journal so you can return to it in 6 months to see what has bloomed.

INTENTION VS GOALS

There is a subtle yet profound difference between setting goals and setting intentions.

Intentions are based in our present purpose and are expansive.

Goals are based in the future, definite, binary, and are therefore more restrictive.

Intention from Old French *entencion*, from Latin intentio(n-) is stretching or purpose.

From intendere (see intend). An intention focuses on our present action and purpose. I.e., She declared an intention to publish her book traditionally with the perfect publisher.

Goal, from its roots in Middle English, is a limit or a boundary. Goals focuses on a future end result. I.e., She set a goal to earn $10k in one month. She set a goal to get published by Forbes.

In intentions, you create specificity with feelings and possibility.

With goals, you create specificity with metrics and measurements.

Feel free to create a combination of intentions and goals in your New Moon rituals, whatever feels right to you.

Most importantly, have fun and leave room for openness and expansiveness to occur.

5 REASONS WHY YOU WANT TO USE THE POWER OF NEW MOONS

· ·

Not sure why you need to do a New Moon Ritual?

Here are 5 reasons why:
1. Make space and time to reset your intentions
2. Get clear on what you really want in this area of your life/business.
3. Cycle through each area of your life/business by following the zodiac seasons.
4. Make manifest your desires through written and spoken word.
5. Get support from well spirit guides you call in.

TIPS ON CREATING YOUR OWN NEW MOON RITUAL

Now that you understand why you should do a New Moon Ritual, here are some tips on creating your own.

⬦ Do make space to plant your seeds of intention.
⬦ Do a New Moon ritual within 72 hours after the Sun and Moon meet, not before.
⬦ Do trust your intuition, there is no right or wrong way to create your ritual.
⬦ Do a ritual by yourself or with loving friends and family.
⬦ Do get clear on what you want and how you want to feel when you receive.
⬦ Do be as specific as possible while leaving room for something better.
⬦ Do use words to ask for what you desire: write or speak aloud.
⬦ Do keep your journal to review in 6 months at the end of this moon cycle.
⬦ Do let go of figuring out the strategies to get what you want.
⬦ Do call in your well ancestors and spirit guides.

DID YOU KNOW?

- ♦ There are 12 or 13 New Moons a year.
- ♦ Each New Moon happens in the same sign as the Sun.
- ♦ As the year progresses, we have a New Moon in each of the signs.
- ♦ If we have a month with two New Moons in the same sign, this is called a Black Moon.
- ♦ A New Moon is the beginning of the cycle between the Sun and the Moon.
- ♦ When the Moon and the Sun meet, the Moon doesn't reflect light back to the Earth and appears dark.
- ♦ Humans for millennia have used the New Moon phase to plant new seeds.
- ♦ Because the spirits that help us mortal humans see all our projects as soilless gardens[1], just like tending a garden, we maximize nature's energy by calling in our well spirit guides and working with the cycles of the Moon in our business projects.
- ♦ An eclipse on a New Moon, the Moon hides the Sun, so it's called a Solar Eclipse
- ♦ Eclipses come in pairs, a Solar Eclipse on a New Moon and a Lunar Eclipse on a Full Moon
- ♦ We normally get 2 pairs of eclipses a year and it happens when the Lunar event happens near the Lunar Nodes

---

1   For more information on working with soilless gardens, read Perelandra Soil-less Garden Companion by Wright.

HOW TO PERSONALIZE
YOUR NEW MOON ACTIVATION

· ·

A Moon becomes "new" when the Sun and Moon meet at the exact same degree.

This degree that the Sun and Moon meet highlight a point in your natal chart.

This highlight point serves as an activation in this area of your life or business. It is where you have the most need to reset and clarify your intentions.

During the year, this activation will travel through the chart, and in most cases, activating each of your twelve houses.

You don't need to know how to fully read or interpret your chart to create a New Moon ritual.

Yet, understanding the houses in your chart will help you customize your New Moon ritual.

Use Your Intuition

Don't worry if you can't get a chart or if this feels too much.

You can always use your intuition and let it guide you when personalizing any New Moon ritual.

There is no wrong way

to set your intention or to create a well-intended ritual!

STEPS TO PERSONALIZE YOUR NEW MOON ACTIVATION

1. Get your natal chart—You can use sites like astro.com or astrology-charts.com or even on my site at thesavvyluminary.com/chart. You'll want to know your birth time for the most accurate chart.

2. Each New Moon happens in a sign on a degree. Find that degree in your chart.

3. Discover the house that contains the degree of the New Moon. That house, in your chart, is being activated.

    ◊ Each of the 12 houses represent an area of your life and business. Throughout a year, a New Moon activation will circle through all 12 houses, allowing you to revisit each area of your business.

    ◊ Interpret for yourself how that area in your business needs/wants to evolve. *What new intentions do you need to set for that area of your business?*

For astro geeks wanting to take it to the next level

1. Notice any other planets or energies in your natal chart that are in **conjunction** (within 5° before or after +/-) to the point activation. That planet and energy will want to be blended in the New Moon activation.
   Interpret for yourself how that energy is blended fully into your intention.

2. Determine the **modality** of the New Moon and look for other energies or planets in the same modality that are within 5° +/-. Any other planets or energies there want a say in the New Moon and will have creative energies that want to be integrated.
   Interpret for yourself how that energy pushes and pulls like creative tension into your intention.

3. Determine the **element** of the New Moon and look for other energies or planets in the same element that are within the 5° +/-. Any other planets or energies there will support and be in flow with your New Moon.
   Interpret for yourself how that energy can support with ease and flow into your intention.

EXAMPLE CHART

In the chart below let's look at the January 2021 New Moon at Capricorn 23°

1. The New Moon in this natal chart is indicated by the star.
2. The New Moon activation happens in the 8H of this chart. 8H in business represents shared resources, debts/liabilities/investments,
3. Notice that Venus is at Capricorn 25°, a **conjunction**, 2 degrees away from the New Moon activation.
    ◊ The energy of Venus as the ruler of both Libra and Taurus represents those astrographics of beauty, values, added value, connection to others.
    ◊ The energy of Venus wants to be blended fully into this Moon intention.
4. Capricorn is a Cardinal modality, Uranus at Libra 27° is adding creative friction. Uranus, the ruler of Aquarius represents those astrographics of breakthrough, individuation, innovation. So those energies will add creative force to this New Moon activation.
5. Capricorn is an Earth element, Mars at Taurus 23° is adding support. Mars, the ruler of Aries represents those astrographics of energy, motivation, drive, initiative. So those energies are supporting this New Moon activation.

Sample interpretation for this New Moon intention.

◊ 8H: This Intentions is best set in the area of the 8H in my business for this New Moon
◊ Venus Conjunction: This intention is blended (conjuncion) with love, values, beauty (Venus).
◊ Uranus Square: This intention seeks integration (square) with individuality and breakthrough (Uranus)..
◊ Mars Trine: This intention is supported (trine) with motivation and drive (Mars).

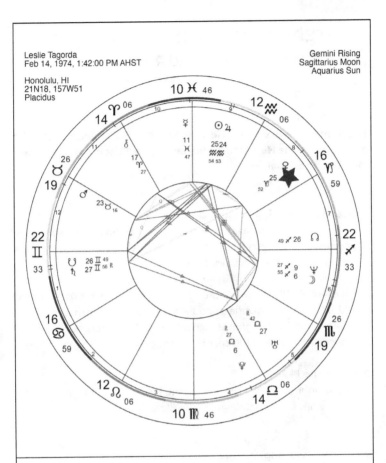

Leslie Tagorda
Feb 14, 1974, 1:42:00 PM AHST

Honolulu, HI
21N18, 157W51
Placidus

Gemini Rising
Sagittarius Moon
Aquarius Sun

Chart Patterns

Type: none
Ruler Asc: Mercury
Asp Pat: Grand Trine

Elements/Modes

Fire	4
Earth	2
Air	8
Water	2
Cardinal	4
Fixed	4
Mutable	8
Strong: Air	

Natal Planets

Sun	☉	25° Aqu 54' 28"	-12.88
Moon	☽	6° Sag 55' 06"	-23.18
Mercury	☿	11° Pis 47'	-5.10
Venus	♀	25° Cap 52'	-13.90
Mars	♂	23° Tau 16'	20.09
Jupiter	♃	24° Aqu 53'	-13.94
Saturn	♄	27° Gem 56'R	22.50
Uranus	♅	27° Lib 42'R	-10.09
Neptune	♆	9° Sag 27'	-20.30
Pluto	♇	6° Lib 27'R	13.04
Chiron	⚷	17° Ari 27'	7.84
N Node	☊	26° Sag 49'	-23.40
Asc.	⊖	22° Gem 33'	
MC	☉	10° Pis 46'	

5 STEPS TO CREATING A NEW MOON RITUAL FOR YOUR BUSINESS

. . . .

The prime time to do your New Moon Ritual is 35 minutes after the exact time of the New Moon. You have up to 72 hours after the New Moon to do a ritual.

1. Clear Space + Bring In Spirit Guides
Clear the clutter physically, mentally, emotionally, and spiritually. Smudge, or burn incense. Center yourself. Call in your spirit guides, your well ancestors, and higher self.

For example, "I'd like to initiate a New Moon ceremony. I'd like to call in the Deva of my business (pause for 10 seconds), Yemayah (pause for 10 seconds), My grandmother (pause for 10 seconds), and my highest self (pause for 10 seconds) to support me in this ceremony."

2. Get In The Flow
Flow in your own way using the element of the Moon. Light a candle, take a walk, take a bath, dance, meditate, journal, etc.

⬥ For Fire moons (Aries, Leo, Sagittarius) try candle gazing, or safely working with fire.
⬥ For Earth moons (Taurus, Virgo, Capricorn) try grounding, dancing, walking barefoot on the earth.
⬥ For Air moons (Gemini, Libra, Aquarius) try meditating, singing, journaling.
⬥ For Water moons (Cancer, Scorpio, Pisces) try swimming, taking a bath, sitting near running water.

3. Dream Big
Get clear on what you desire. Go big, let go of the "hows" and write it down!

4. Ask For What You Want

After journaling and deciding what you desire to bring forth, ask your spirit guides and highest self, out loud or on paper, for your intentions.

For example: "I, __name__, would like to plant the seeds to receive _____."

- ◊ What do you want?
- ◊ Why do you want it?
- ◊ How do you want to feel as/when you manifest it?

5. Give Thanks & Release

Express your gratitude to your guides and release them.

For example: "Thank you for expanding my horizons on my True Path by planting the seeds of my intention so that it may serve me and others for the highest good of all. May you be free to go forth into your world to complete your purpose and support my purpose. I now release my highest self, my grandmother, Yemayah and the Deva of my business." (Release them in the reverse order to which you brought them in, no need to pause.)

CLOSE THE CEREMONY

BONUS: Cultivate the energy

Give forward the energy you want to cultivate. For example, if you want to eat more healthily, help someone else eat more healthy. It doesn't have to be complicated. Simple ways to pass the energy you want to cultivate out into the world. Gratitude and appreciation is the secret.

12 NEW MOONS OF 2021

· ·

Mark your calendars!

January 12/13, 2021 Capricorn 23°
January 12 - 9:00 PM PT / 12:00 AM ET
January 13 - 4:00 AM GMT / 4:00 PM AEST / 6:00 PM NZST

February 11/12, 2021 Aquarius 23°
February 11 - 11:06 AM PT / 2:06 PM ET / 7:08 PM GMT
February 12 - 5:06 AM AEST / 8:06 AM NZST

March 13 2021, 2021 Pisces 23°
March 13 - 2:21 AM PT / 5:21 AM ET / 10:21 AM GMT / 8:21 PM / 11:21 PM

April 11/12, 2021 Aries 22°
April 11 7:31 PM PT / 10:31 PM ET
April 12 2:31 AM GMT / 12:31 PM AEST / 2:31 PM NZST

May 11/12, 2021 Taurus 21°
May 11 - 12:00 PM PT / 3:00 PM ET
May 12 - 7:00 PM GMT / 5:00 AM AEST / 7:00 AM NZST

June 10, 2021 Gemini 19°
June 10 - 3:53 AM PT / 6:53 AM ET / 10:53 AM GMT 8:53 PM AEST
10:53 PM NZST

July 9/10, 2021 Cancer 18°
   July 9 - 6:17 PM PT / 9:17 PM ET
   July 10 - 1:17 AM GMT / 11:17 AM AEST / 1:17 PM NZST

August 8/9, 2021 Leo 16°
   August 8 - 2021 6:50 AM PT / 9:50 AM ET / 1:50 PM GMT / 11:50PM AEST
   August 9 - 1:50 AM NZST

September 7/8, 2021 Virgo 14°
   September 7 - 5:52 PM PT / 8:52 PM ET
   September 8 - 12:52 AM GMT / 10:52 AM AEST / 12:52 PM NZST

October 6/7, 2021 Libra 13°
   October 6 - 4:05 AM PT / 7:05 AM ET / 11:05 AM GMT / 9:05 PM AEST
   October 7 - 2:05 AM NZST

November 4/5, 2021 Scorpio 12°
   November 4 - 2:15 PM PT / 5:15 PM ET / 9:15 PM GMT
   November 5 - 7:15 AM AEST / 10:15 AM NZST

December 3/4, 2021 Sagittarius 12°
   December 3 - 11:43 PM PT
   December 4 - 2:43 AM ET / 7:43 AM GMT / 5:43 PM NZST PT
   8:34 AM NZST

NEW MOON JANUARY 2021
CAPRICORN 23°

· ·

Today I plant the seeds to define redefine success and my ultimate mission in my business and brand

January 12/13, 2021
January 12 9:00 PM PT / 12:00 AM ET
January 13 4:00 AM GMT / 4:00 PM AEST / 6:00 PM NZST

Look back to this time a year ago, the world as we knew it began to unravel and come to a standstill. And now we are ready to move forward; ready to continue to dismantle the old while putting in the new framework for an equitable future.

This is where your business comes in. The cosmos wants you, spiritual entrepreneur, to reinvision what success in business means to you. You get to decide the impact you want to have, the structures and systems for sustainable growth, and the future forward vision you'd like to live in your business.

You are the creator of your ultimate mission.

Decide today what success and value looks like to you in your spiritual business. On your individualistic terms.

Cosmic Notes for the Astro Geeks

◊ First New Moon of the Year Pluto conjunction—very intense and great for deep transformation.
◊ Majority of the energies tied up in stellium between leading Venus Capricorn 5° and Mercury Aquarius 7°.
◊ All planets in a cluster within tight trine between Venus and Uranus.
◊ Saturn/Jupiter/Mercury conjunct in Aquarius fixed square to Mars and Uranus in Taurus.

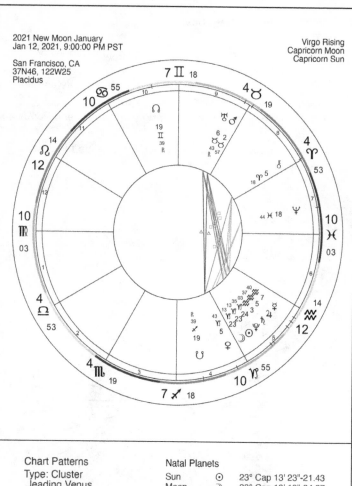

2021 New Moon January
Jan 12, 2021, 9:00:00 PM PST

San Francisco, CA
37N46, 122W25
Placidus

Virgo Rising
Capricorn Moon
Capricorn Sun

Chart Patterns

Type: Cluster
leading Venus
Ruler Asc: Mercury

Elements/Modes

Fire	1
Earth	10
Air	4
Water	1

Cardinal	7
Fixed	5
Mutable	4

Strong: Earth

Natal Planets

Sun	☉	23° Cap 13' 23"	-21.43
Moon	☽	23° Cap 13' 19"	-24.27
Mercury	☿	7° Aqu 40'	-20.09
Venus	♀	5° Cap 43'	-23.17
Mars	♂	2° Tau 57'	13.50
Jupiter	♃	5° Aqu 37'	-19.35
Saturn	♄	3° Aqu 03'	-19.86
Uranus	♅	6° Tau 43'R	13.33
Neptune	♆	18° Pis 44'	-5.44
Pluto	♇	24° Cap 35'	-22.39
Chiron	⚷	5° Ari 18'	4.40
N Node	☊	19° Gem 39'R	23.03
Asc.	⊖	10° Vir 03'	
MC	①	7° Gem 18'	

24

Today I plant the seeds to redefine success and my ultimate mission in my business's:

 1H: Brand and leadership ability
 2H: Values and how I add value to my customers
 3H: Communications and how I promote my brand
 4H: Emotional groundedness and home base
 5H: Creative joy, play and purpose
 6H: Day to day operations, automations and ability to delegate
 7H: Collaboration with my ideal customers and co-creators
 8H: Ability to transform and heal
 9H: Expansion and ideal vision
10H: Ultimate mission in my work
11H: Social impact and community building
12H: Ability to restore, retreat and surrender

PERSONALIZE YOUR NEW MOON RITUAL

◊ What house is being activated? What area of my business is available to add to my intention?

◊ Do I have any energies/planets within 5° of Capricorn 23°? If yes, how do those energies want to blend in?

◊ Do I have any other Cardinal energies within 5° of, Aries, Cancer, Libra 23°? If yes, how do those energies want to add creative friction?

◊ Do I have any other Earth energies within 5° of Taurus or Virgo 23°? If yes, how do those energies want to support my new moon intention?

JOURNALING PROMPTS TO DISTILL YOUR INTENTION:

1. What kind of success do you want in your business in this new year?
2. What kind of visibility do you want in your business this year?
3. What kind of impact do I want my business to make in the next year?
4. What do you want your ultimate mission in your business to be?
5. What new offerings do you want to deliver in your business in 2021?
6. What results do you want your customers to achieve when working with you?
7. What recognition and accomplishment do you want to gain?

_____

_____

_____

_____

_____

_____

_____

_____

_____

_____

Today _____
DATE

I, _____ ,
NAME

plant the seeds of defining success

in my business and brand:

[[Write your New Moon intention and speak it out loud.
Return to this often.]]

What do I want?

_____

_____

Why do I want this?

_____

_____

How do I want to feel as/when I manifest this?

_____

_____

NEW MOON FEBRUARY 2021
AQUARIUS 23°
. . . .

Today I plant the seeds to call in my community to create social impact with my business and brand.

February 11/12, 2021
February 11 11:06 AM PT / 2:06 PM ET / 7:08 PM GMT
February 12 5:06 AM AEST / 8:06 AM NZST

Social impact and innovation has a new meaning and feel for you, especially since Mercury Retrograde has been giving you the space to rethink what it all means. As a spiritual business, you have your own version of innovation. Perhaps it's tapping into ancient wisdom or technologies and making it new for modern practitioners. Or the impact you make is meant to serve less people in more intimate ways vs going big and large like the days of the profittering past. Or even reinventing how you personally take care of Mother Earth and the Environment

However Aquarian ideals show up for you, whether it be community impact, humanitarian ideals, social justice for all, equitable futures, or even your personal hopes and dreams, you get a chance to rewrite your story in the way you do business and how your business impacts the environment. .

You feel this need to innovate. You feel this need to call in your greater community because you can't do this alone. Decide today what groundbreaking social impact you want to make in your spiritual business.

Cosmic Notes for the Astro Geeks

- ◊ Mercury Retrograde in Aquarius: Realizations about the future and community.
- ◊ Another cluster/Stellium in Aquarius fixed square to Mars and Uranus in Taurus: Future forward urgency around new technologies for the environment.
- ◊ Aquarius stellium and fixed energies. Organizing your future facing values

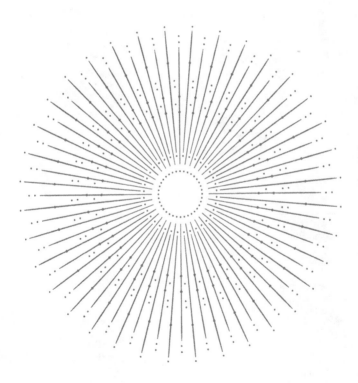

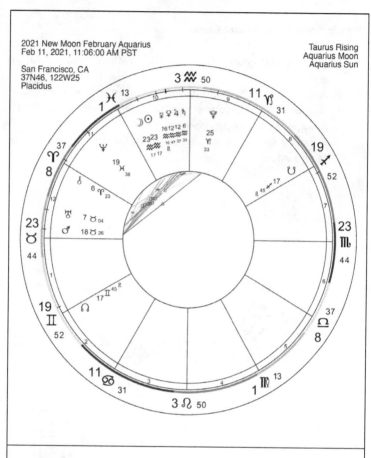

2021 New Moon February Aquarius
Feb 11, 2021, 11:06:00 AM PST

Taurus Rising
Aquarius Moon
Aquarius Sun

San Francisco, CA
37N46, 122W25
Placidus

Chart Patterns		Natal Planets			
Type: Cluster		Sun	☉	23° Aqu 16' 45"	-13.75
leading Pluto		Moon	☽	23° Aqu 16' 57"	-18.08
Ruler Asc: Venus		Mercury	☿	16° Aqu 16'R	-12.46
		Venus	♀	12° Aqu 47'	-17.91
Elements/Modes		Mars	♂	18° Tau 26'	18.62
Fire	1	Jupiter	♃	12° Aqu 37'	-17.54
Earth	5	Saturn	♄	6° Aqu 33'	-19.05
Air	9	Uranus	♅	7° Tau 04'	13.46
Water	1	Neptune	♆	19° Pis 38'	-5.08
		Pluto	♇	25° Cap 33'	-22.26
Cardinal	2	Chiron	⚷	6° Ari 23'	4.75
Fixed	13	N Node	☊	17° Gem 45'R	22.87
Mutable	1	Asc.	⊖	23° Tau 44'	
Strong: Air		MC	①	3° Aqu 50'	

Today I plant the seeds to call in my larger community and platform through my business's:

  1H: Brand awareness and innovative leadership
  2H: Equitable and social justice values
  3H: Communications and how I share knowledge
  4H: Emotional groundedness and safe communities
  5H: Creative joy, pleasure and purpose
  6H: mart automations and ability to delegate with bots
  7H: Collaboration with my future forward co-creators
  8H: Innovative ways to transform and leverage liabilities
  9H: Expansive vision and journeying work
10H: Ultimate mission in my humanitarian work
11H: Greater social impact and community building
12H: Ability to create ease and flow for all

PERSONALIZE YOUR NEW MOON RITUAL

◊ What house is being activated? What area of my business is available to add to my intention?

◊ Do I have any energies/planets within 5° of Aquarius 23°? If yes, how do those energies want to blend in?

◊ Do I have any other Fixed energies within 5° of, Taurus, Leo, Scorpio 23°? If yes, how do those energies want to add creative friction?

◊ Do I have any other Air energies within 5° of Gemini or Libra 23°? If yes, how do those energies want to support my new moon intention?

JOURNALING PROMPTS TO DISTILL YOUR INTENTION:

1. What kinds of people do you want to bring together in your platform and communities?
2. What do you want to build in your social communities and platforms?
3. What do you want to be known for in your larger networks?
4. What does showing up in your community look like for you?
5. What kind of innovation do you want to build in your industry?
6. What do you want social equity and DEI work to do in your business?
7. What do you want to give back through your business?

_____

_____

_____

_____

_____

_____

_____

_____

_____

_____

Today _____
DATE

I, _____ ,
NAME

plant the seeds of calling in my community to

create social impact with my business and brand:

[[Write your New Moon intention and speak it out loud.
Return to this often.]]

What do I want?

_____

_____

Why do I want this?

_____

_____

How do I want to feel as/when I manifest this?

_____

_____

Today I plant the seeds to bring in more ease and flow with connection to my Divine in my business and brand.

March 13, 2021
2:21 AM PT / 5:21 AM ET / 10:21 AM GMT / 8:21 PM / 11:21 PM

Beautiful and dreamy, this New Moon is your connection to the Divine. Imagine your most divine self, showing you the past, present, and future vision. She has chosen this path that you are on of spiritual entrepreneurship. Goddess, you know entrepreneurship is for the courageous of heart. And the most courageous of hearts are those that can hold vast empathy and compassion.

When you dream of the visions for your business, how simply can you attain this vision? How in ease can you work? And what can you accomplish when in flow?

What if your spirituality is the way to innovate and make impact in your business?

Decide today what ease and flow looks like to you in your spiritual business. What does your connection to Spirit want you to see?

Cosmic Notes for the Astro Geeks

- ✧ New Moon Conjunct Neptune
- ✧ Pisces Stellium
- ✧ Cluster in Aquarius
- ✧ Sextile with Pluto

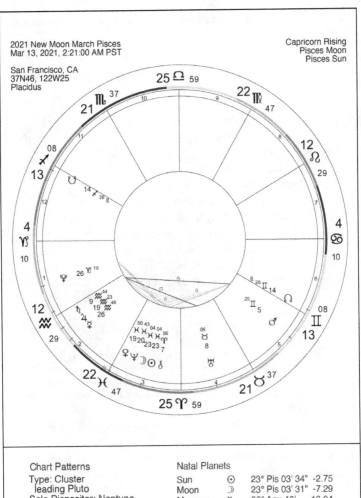

2021 New Moon March Pisces
Mar 13, 2021, 2:21:00 AM PST

San Francisco, CA
37N46, 122W25
Placidus

Capricorn Rising
Pisces Moon
Pisces Sun

Chart Patterns	Natal Planets		
Type: Cluster leading Pluto	Sun	☉	23° Pis 03' 34" -2.75
Sole Dispositor: Neptune	Moon	☽	23° Pis 03' 31" -7.29
Ruler Asc: Saturn	Mercury	☿	26° Aqu 46' -13.94
	Venus	♀	19° Pis 50' -5.34
Elements/Modes	Mars	♂	5° Gem 25' 22.65
Fire 1	Jupiter	♃	19° Aqu 23' -15.58
Earth 4	Saturn	♄	9° Aqu 44' -18.27
Air 5	Uranus	♅	8° Tau 06' 13.81
Water 6	Neptune	♆	20° Pis 43' -4.65
	Pluto	♇	26° Cap 19' -22.17
Cardinal 5	Chiron	⚷	7° Ari 56' 5.31
Fixed 4	N Node	☊	14° Gem 28'R 22.53
Mutable 7	Asc.	⊖	4° Cap 10'
Strong: Water	MC	①	25° Lib 59'

39

Today I plant the seeds to bring more ease and flow and connection to the Divine/Highest Self in my business's:

  1H: Brand identity and leadership style
  2H: Values and sales promise
  3H: Communication and promotional style
  4H: Safe spaces I create for customers
  5H: Creative process and passion in projects
  6H: Day to day operations and business wellness
  7H: Commitment to my ideal customers and contractors
  8H: Money stories and relationship with shared resources
  9H: Visioning and global reach
10H: Delivering your best work
11H: Larger community outreach and platform building
12H: Restoration and completing of unfinished business

PERSONALIZE YOUR NEW MOON RITUAL

◊ What house is being activated? What area of my business is available to add to my intention?

◊ Do I have any energies/planets within 5° of Pisces 23°? If yes, how do those energies want to blend in?

◊ Do I have any other Mutable energies within 5° of, Gemini, Virgo, Sagittarius 23°? If yes, how do those energies want to add creative friction?

◊ Do I have any other Water energies within 5° of Cancer or Scorpio 23°? If yes, how do those energies want to support my new moon intention?

JOURNALING PROMPTS TO DISTILL YOUR INTENTION:

1. What do you want it to feel like to always hear and trust your higher self?
2. What is the vision of your business that your highest self wants you to have?
3. How can you bring more spirituality into your business for support?
4. What do you want to reform in your business?
5. What in your business do you want to simplify for ease and flow?
6. What do you want your dreams to tell you about your business vision?

_____

_____

_____

_____

_____

_____

_____

_____

_____

_____

_____

Today _____
DATE

I, _____ ,
NAME

plant the seeds of calling in my community
to bring in more ease and flow with
the Divine into my business and brand:

[[Write your New Moon intention and speak it out loud.
Return to this often.]]

What do I want?

_____

_____

Why do I want this?

_____

_____

How do I want to feel as/when I manifest this?

_____

_____

NEW MOON APRIL 2021
ARIES 22°

· ·

*Today I plant the seeds to call in my
authentic leadership style to be a trailblazer
in my business and brand.*

April 11/12, 2021
April 11 7:31 PM PT / 10:31 PM ET
April 12 2:31 AM GMT / 12:31 PM AEST / 2:31 PM NZST

In Astrology, the New Moon in Aries, shortly after Equinox, is like a New Year celebration—a rebirth as we begin again at the first sign of the zodiac. A time of revival and renewal, and in your business, reviving how you want to show up.

Aries is bold and takes lead, and in our chart shows us where in our business we need to show up boldly. And the sign on the rising (aka ascendant) sign on the first house cusp is the energy we are born to embody in our leadership style and brand identity.

This is your chance to love the leader you are born to be and fall in love again with your brand identity. If you feel good, you become irresistible to your soul customers.

Decide today what leadership and brand identity you want in your spiritual business. The sweet spot is the intersection of what you want and what others love in you.

Cosmic Notes for the Astro Geeks

- ✧ New moon conjunct Venus: Love your leadership and brand style.
- ✧ New moon sextile Mars, Mars Square Neptune: Taking inspired and spiritual action has creative rewards.
- ✧ Square Pluto: If you don't choose how you lead, Pluto will choose for you, it may not be what you want.
- ✧ Sextile Jupiter: Be grateful for what you have and the bigger you can dream, the bigger the creative rewards.

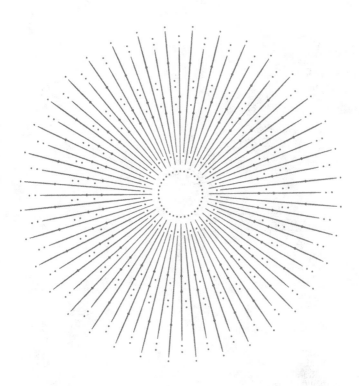

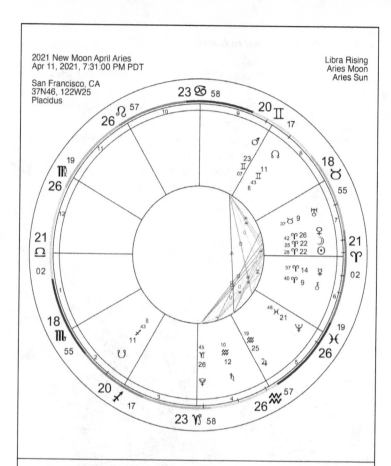

2021 New Moon April Aries
Apr 11, 2021, 7:31:00 PM PDT

San Francisco, CA
37N46, 122W25
Placidus

Libra Rising
Aries Moon
Aries Sun

Chart Patterns

Type: Bowl
  leading Pluto
Ruler Asc: Venus

Elements/Modes

Fire	7
Earth	2
Air	5
Water	2

Cardinal	11
Fixed	3
Mutable	2
Strong: Fire	

Natal Planets

Sun	☉	22° Ari 24' 42"	8.72
Moon	☽	22° Ari 24' 48"	5.11
Mercury	☿	14° Ari 57'	4.45
Venus	♀	26° Ari 42'	9.36
Mars	♂	23° Gem 07'	24.73
Jupiter	♃	25° Aqu 19'	-13.72
Saturn	♄	12° Aqu 10'	-17.66
Uranus	♅	9° Tau 37'	14.30
Neptune	♆	21° Pis 48'	-4.24
Pluto	♇	26° Cap 45'	-22.15
Chiron	⚷	9° Ari 40'	5.96
N Node	☊	11° Gem 43'R	22.18
Asc.	⊖	21° Lib 02'	
MC	⌾	23° Can 58'	

HOUSE ACTIVATIONS TO PERSONALIZE YOUR NEW MOON RITUAL

Today I plant the seeds to show up in my business in my authentic leadership style as a:

1H: Natural born, decisive self-directed leader
2H: Worthy, resourceful , natural entrepreneur
3H: Action-oriented orator, writer or thought leader
4H: Nurturing, family and community-centered matriarch
5H: Heart-centered, joyful, and charismatic director
6H: Organized, systematic, effective commander in chief
7H: Committed partner, outgoing, connector
8H: Transformative, trusting, and authentic arbiter
9H: Expansive global explorer, and visionary trend setter
10H: Bold personal brand and professional pioneer
11H: Community builder and social impact maker
12H: Consciously connected, empathetic, intuitive sage

PERSONALIZE YOUR NEW MOON RITUAL

◇ What house is being activated? What area of my business is available to add to my intention?
◇ Do I have any energies/planets within 5° of Aries 22? If yes, how do those energies want to blend in?
◇ Do I have any other Cardinal energies within 5° of, Cancer, Libra, Capricorn 22°? If yes, how do those energies want to add creative friction?
◇ Do I have any other Fire energies within 5° of Leo or Sagittarius 22°? If yes, how do those energies want to support my new moon intention?

JOURNALING PROMPTS TO DISTILL YOUR INTENTION:

1. Where in your business do you need to be seen as the leader?
2. What kind of leader do you want to be vs what you were taught you should be?
3. What does initiative look like for you in your business?
4. How do you want to feel as you take initiative?
5. How do you want others to feel about your business?
6. What do you want your brand identity to look and feel like?
7. How do you want others to feel about your business and brand?
8. What do you want in your personal style to reflect your leadership ability?

_____

_____

_____

_____

_____

_____

_____

_____

_____

_____

_____

Today _____
DATE

I, _____ ,
NAME

plant the seeds of authentic leadership

in my business and brand:

[[Write your New Moon intention and speak it out loud.
Return to this often.]]

What do I want?

_____

_____

Why do I want this?

_____

_____

How do I want to feel as/when I manifest this?

_____

_____

NEW MOON MAY 2021
TAURUS 21°

. . . .

*Today I plant the seeds to call in my
impactful value and abundant profit
in my business and brand.*

May 11/12, 2021
May 11 12:00 PM PT / 3:00 PM ET
May 12 7:00 PM GMT / 5:00 AM AEST / 7:00 AM NZST

Abundance, profit, resources, value...whatever you call it, we need it in our physical life here on Mother Earth. Each of us wants different things and has our own reasons for desiring moola. It's up to us to understand what we want and what allows us to gain it. Equally, the value that we deliver to our customers has different meanings and it's up to us to deliver and define our value.

There are many things that go into our ability to earn the resources we need and at the core is how we value ourselves and what we offer in the world. The first step is to see and ground your value. If you don't value yourself or your offerings, no one else will.

Decide today what abundance and value-add looks like to you in your spiritual business. On your individualistic expansive terms.

Cosmic Notes for the Astro Geeks

- ✧ New Moon Wide conjunction with Uranus
- ✧ New Moon Sextile with Neptune
- ✧ New Moon Wide square with Juptier
- ✧ New Moon Trine with Pluto
- ✧ Saturn trine Mercury
- ✧ Mars square Chiron

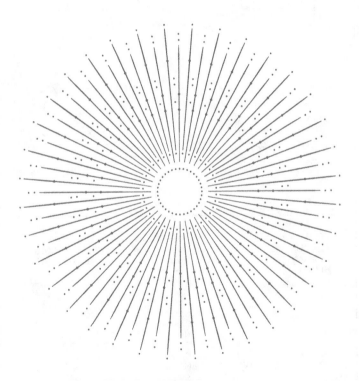

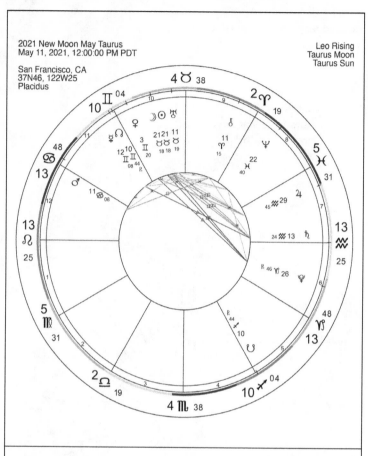

2021 New Moon May Taurus
May 11, 2021, 12:00:00 PM PDT

San Francisco, CA
37N46, 122W25
Placidus

Leo Rising
Taurus Moon
Taurus Sun

Chart Patterns

Type: Bowl
  leading Pluto
Ruler Asc: Sun

Elements/Modes

Fire	3
Earth	7
Air	4
Water	2

Cardinal	3
Fixed	10
Mutable	3

Strong: Earth

Natal Planets

Sun	☉	21° Tau 17' 51"	18.08
Moon	☽	21° Tau 17' 58"	16.39
Mercury	☿	12° Gem 08'	24.68
Venus	♀	3° Gem 20'	20.90
Mars	♂	11° Can 08'	24.38
Jupiter	♃	29° Aqu 45'	-12.29
Saturn	♄	13° Aqu 24'	-17.37
Uranus	♅	11° Tau 19'	14.83
Neptune	♆	22° Pis 40'	-3.91
Pluto	♇	26° Cap 46'R	-22.21
Chiron	⚷	11° Ari 15'	6.58
N Node	☊	10° Gem 44'R	22.05
Asc.	⊖	13° Leo 25'	
MC	⊕	4° Tau 38'	

HOUSE ACTIVATIONS TO PERSONALIZE YOUR NEW MOON RITUAL

I plant the seeds to manifest impactful value and abundant profit in my business's:

- 1H: Brand identity and wealth-building leadership
- 2H: Brand promises and added value that elevates customer's finances
- 3H: Marketing that expresses pleasurable, abundant and steady outcomes
- 4H: Home base, safe communities and real estate (land) investments
- 5H: Fun, artistic and creative investments that are heart-felt
- 6H: Day-to-day systems and business health that enable effective profitability
- 7H: Monetizable partnerships and collaborations with win-win-win results
- 8H: Investing in and sustainable leveraging of other people's resources
- 9H: Expanding purpose by giving thanks for and giving back of material wealth
- 10H: Professionally recognized expertise and influential status
- 11H: Lucrative community and platform that supports environmental causes
- 12H: Charitable opportunities that give back and provide stability to others

PERSONALIZE YOUR NEW MOON RITUAL

- ◊ What house is being activated? What area of my business is available to add to my intention?
- ◊ Do I have any energies/planets within 5° of Taurus 21°? If yes, how do those energies want to blend in?
- ◊ Do I have any other Fixed energies within 5° of, Leo, Scorpio, Aquarius 21°? If yes, how do those energies want to add creative friction?
- ◊ Do I have any other Earth energies within 5° of Virgo or Capricorn 21°? If yes, how do those energies want to support my new moon intention?

JOURNALING PROMPTS TO DISTILL YOUR INTENTION:

1. What does abundance and profitability feel like to you?
2. Why do you want to be abundantly profitable?
3. What do you want to spend your money on and invest in your business?
4. What treats do you want to buy for yourself?
5. What are your business values and how do you want others to experience them?
6. What about your business do you absolutely love?
7. What do you need to believe about you and your business in order to be abundantly profitable?
8. What do you want to promise and accomplish for your customers? (This is your value add.)
9. What do you want the transformational impact of your business to be?

_____

_____

_____

_____

_____

_____

_____

_____

Today _____
DATE

I, _____ ,
NAME

plant the seeds of impactful value and

abundant profitability in my business:

[[Write your New Moon intention and speak it out loud.
Return to this often.]]

What do I want?

_____

_____

Why do I want this?

_____

_____

How do I want to feel as/when I manifest this?

_____

_____

NEW MOON JUNE 2021
GEMINI 19° (SOLAR ECLIPSE)

. . . .

Today I plant the seeds to redefine powerful clear messaging and engaging dialog in my business and brand.

June 10, 2021
3:53 AM PT / 6:53 AM ET / 10:53 AM GMT / 8:53 PM AEST / 10:53 PM NZST

The ruler of Gemini, Mercury, is at the halfway point of this second retrograde season. And we have a Solar Eclipse. Overload of information! While you may not be able to find the exact words or get clear on your exact thoughts, if you go one level below those thoughts, you do KNOW how you want your message to be heard. You do know why you want your brand voice to be heard. And you do know the impact you want your message to have in your circles.

It's a powerful New Moon with all the other cosmic support to rethink your brand voice and all that it means.

Decide today the impact you want your message and brand voice to have and be known for in your spiritual business. Rethink what is possible.

Cosmic Notes for the Astro Geeks

- ◇ New Moon Eclipse
- ◇ New Moon conjunct Mercury Rx - a day before combust
- ◇ Mercury Retrograde in Gemini
- ◇ New Moon Square Neptune
- ◇ New Moon trine Saturn

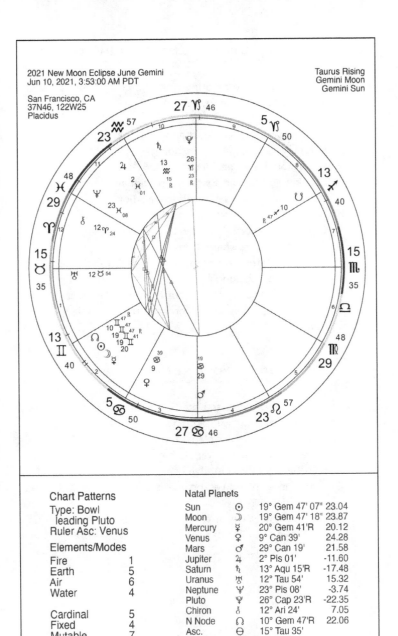

2021 New Moon Eclipse June Gemini
Jun 10, 2021, 3:53:00 AM PDT

Taurus Rising
Gemini Moon
Gemini Sun

San Francisco, CA
37N46, 122W25
Placitus

Chart Patterns

Type: Bowl
  leading Pluto
Ruler Asc: Venus

Elements/Modes

Fire	1
Earth	5
Air	6
Water	4

Cardinal	5
Fixed	4
Mutable	7

Strong: Air

Natal Planets

Planet		Position	
Sun	☉	19° Gem 47' 07"	23.04
Moon	☽	19° Gem 47' 18"	23.87
Mercury	☿	20° Gem 41'R	20.12
Venus	♀	9° Can 39'	24.28
Mars	♂	29° Can 19'	21.58
Jupiter	♃	2° Pis 01'	-11.60
Saturn	♄	13° Aqu 15'R	-17.48
Uranus	♅	12° Tau 54'	15.32
Neptune	♆	23° Pis 08'	-3.74
Pluto	♇	26° Cap 23'R	-22.35
Chiron	⚷	12° Ari 24'	7.05
N Node	☊	10° Gem 47'R	22.06
Asc.	⊖	15° Tau 35'	
MC	⏀	27° Cap 46'	

Today I plant the seeds to redefine powerful clear communications and engaging dialog through my business's:

1H: Leading your brand with sharing your big message
2H: Shared values-focused messaging
3H: Witty stories and teachings
4H: Speaking up to hold space for emotional nurturing
5H: Fun creative writing and communication style
6H: Daily communication systems that serve others
7H: Collaborative partnerships with shared ideas
8H: Powerful and transparent fine print
9H: Global reach through an expansive vision and shared beliefs
10H: Professional speaking and thought leadership
11H: Greater community and platform of shared impact
12H: Imaginative nonverbal communications and language in flow

PERSONALIZE YOUR NEW MOON RITUAL

◊ What house is being activated? What area of my business is available to add to my intention?

◊ Do I have any energies/planets within 5° of Gemini 19°? If yes, how do those energies want to blend in?

◊ Do I have any other Mutable energies within 5° of, Virgo, Sagittarius, Pisces 19°? If yes, how do those energies want to add creative friction?

◊ Do I have any other Air energies within 5° of Libra or Aquarius 19°? If yes, how do those energies want to support my new moon intention?

JOURNALING PROMPTS TO DISTILL YOUR INTENTION:

1. What do you want your message to effectively communicate?
2. What do you want the result of your clear message to be?
3. How do you want people to feel when they hear your message?
4. What do you want people to do when they hear your message?
5. Who do you want to start up a dialog with your brand communications?
6. How do you want your brand messages to be heard?
7. What about your core messaging do you want to evolve?

Today _____
DATE

I, _____ ,
NAME

plant the seeds of redefine powerful
clear messaging and engaging dialog
in my business:

[[Write your New Moon intention and speak it out loud.
Return to this often.]]

What do I want?

_____

_____

Why do I want this?

_____

_____

How do I want to feel as/when I manifest this?

_____

_____

Today I plant the seeds to nurture safe spaces and soft power in my business and brand.

July 9/0, 2021
July 9 6:17 PM PT / 9:17 PM ET
July 10 1:17 AMGMT / 11:17 AM AEST / 1:17 PM NZST

Emotional security is the foundation to your achievement and success. If your emotional center is not rooted, there is nothing you can care for or nurture in your life or business in a meaningful way. Others may see you as successful, but you don't feel it. Or you chase success without creating a safe inner landscape.

This goes for your customers too. In creating safe spaces for their success and results to happen. This is the space that you create with Cancer energy. True healing and success can only happen in these safe spaces.

And creating safe spaces doesn't take muscle power, it takes soft power. Cancer, a water sign, is the ultimate soft power. Nothing is softer than water but there is nothing that can withstand it. What does soft power look and feel like for you? How can you use this in your business to move mountains?

Decide today what emotional security and safe spaces look like and do for you in your spiritual business. On your loving and soft-powered terms.

Cosmic Notes for the Astro Geeks

- ♦ Venus conjunct Mars, Square Uranus

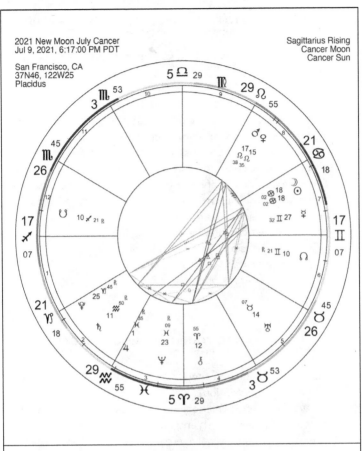

2021 New Moon July Cancer
Jul 9, 2021, 6:17:00 PM PDT

San Francisco, CA
37N46, 122W25
Placidus

Sagittarius Rising
Cancer Moon
Cancer Sun

Chart Patterns

Type: none
Ruler Asc: Jupiter
Asp Pat: T-Square
  to Uranus

Elements/Modes

Fire	5
Earth	2
Air	3
Water	6

Cardinal	7
Fixed	4
Mutable	5
Strong: Water	

Natal Planets

Planet		Position	
Sun	☉	18° Can 01' 41"	22.22
Moon	☽	18° Can 01' 53"	25.36
Mercury	☿	27° Gem 32'	21.40
Venus	♀	15° Leo 35'	17.75
Mars	♂	17° Leo 38'	16.69
Jupiter	♃	1° Pis 35'R	-11.89
Saturn	♄	11° Aqu 50'R	-17.94
Uranus	♅	14° Tau 07'	15.68
Neptune	♆	23° Pis 09'R	-3.76
Pluto	♇	25° Cap 45'R	-22.52
Chiron	⚷	12° Ari 55'	7.27
N Node	☊	10° Gem 21'R	21.99
Asc.	⊖	17° Sag 07'	
MC	①	5° Lib 29'	

67

Today I plant the seeds to nurture safe spaces and soft power in my business's:

  1H: Brand identity and leadership role
  2H: Values and added value to my customers
  3H: Communications and how I promote my brand
  4H: Emotional groundedness for others and home base
  5H: Creative joy, play and heart-centered purpose
  6H: Day to day operations, automations and ability to delegate
  7H: Collaboration with my ideal customers and co-creators
  8H: Ability to transform and heal
  9H: Purpose, vision and philosophy
10H: Ultimate mission and delivery in my work
11H: Social impact and community building
12H: Ability to offer restoration and retreat

PERSONALIZE YOUR NEW MOON RITUAL

◇ What house is being activated? What area of my business is available to add to my intention?

◇ Do I have any energies/planets within 5° of Cancer 18°? If yes, how do those energies want to blend in?

◇ Do I have any other Cardinal energies within 5° of, Aries, Libra, Capricorn 18°? If yes, how do those energies want to add creative friction?

◇ Do I have any other Water energies within 5° of Scorpio or Pisces 18°? If yes, how do those energies want to support my new moon intention?

JOURNALING PROMPTS TO DISTILL YOUR INTENTION:

1. What about your emotions do you see as a strength?
2. What do you want to empower in your business through your emotional intelligence and soft power?
3. What boundaries do you want to create for emotional security in your business (knowing that emotional security allows you to succeed and rise?)
4. What self care practices and boundaries do you want to create in your business to prevent burnout?
5. What is your desired inner narrative that allows you to be empowered?
6. What self-assurances can you give/make/create for yourself?

Today _____
DATE

I, _____ ,
NAME

plant the seeds of safe spaces

and soft power in my business:

[[Write your New Moon intention and speak it out loud.
Return to this often.]]

What do I want?

_____

_____

Why do I want this?

_____

_____

How do I want to feel as/when I manifest this?

_____

_____

NEW MOON AUGUST 2021 LEO 16°

· ·

*Today I plant the seeds to confidently shine
brighter with heart-centered purpose in my
business and brand.*

August 8/9, 2021
August 8, 2021 6:50 AM PT / 9:50 AM ET / 1:50 PM GMT / 11:50PM AEST
August 9 1:50 AM NZST

Are you having fun in your business? Are you doing things that allow you to show up in your brilliance, shining brightly like the luminary you are born to be. Living and working with purpose and vitality?

If you aren't doing things that bring you pleasure and joy, then why are you doing what you do? As a spiritual entrepreneur, you understand that pleasure is directly tied to your health and success. So you owe it to yourself to bring in joy and shine brighter in your work.

Check in with your spirit to understand if you're leading with your heart. And shake off all the shoulds and expectations of others. You call the shots.

Decide today what confidence and shining brightly look like for you in your spiritual business. On your individual heart-centered terms.

Cosmic Notes for the Astro Geeks

- ♦ New moon square Uranus
- ♦ Venus opposite Neptune

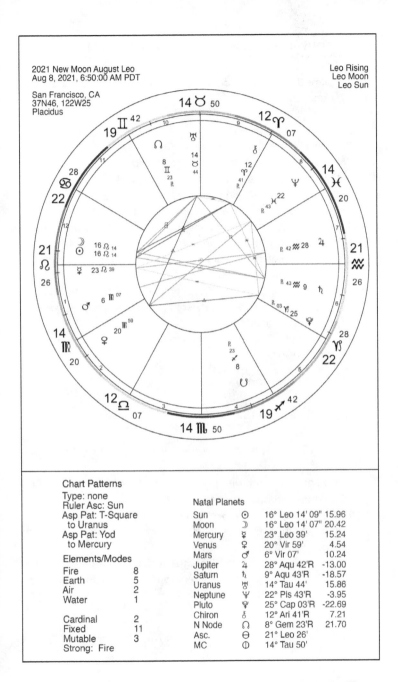

2021 New Moon August Leo
Aug 8, 2021, 6:50:00 AM PDT

San Francisco, CA
37N46, 122W25
Placidus

Leo Rising
Leo Moon
Leo Sun

Chart Patterns

Type: none
Ruler Asc: Sun
Asp Pat: T-Square
  to Uranus
Asp Pat: Yod
  to Mercury

Elements/Modes

Fire	8
Earth	5
Air	2
Water	1

Cardinal	2
Fixed	11
Mutable	3

Strong: Fire

Natal Planets

Sun	☉	16° Leo 14' 09"	15.96
Moon	☽	16° Leo 14' 07"	20.42
Mercury	☿	23° Leo 39'	15.24
Venus	♀	20° Vir 59'	4.54
Mars	♂	6° Vir 07'	10.24
Jupiter	♃	28° Aqu 42'R	-13.00
Saturn	♄	9° Aqu 43'R	-18.57
Uranus	♅	14° Tau 44'	15.86
Neptune	♆	22° Pis 43'R	-3.95
Pluto	♇	25° Cap 03'R	-22.69
Chiron	⚷	12° Ari 41'R	7.21
N Node	☊	8° Gem 23'R	21.70
Asc.	⊖	21° Leo 26'	
MC	①	14° Tau 50'	

73

Today I plant the seeds to confidently shine brighter with heart-centered purpose in...

 1H: How I show up and lead
 2H: What I value and how I add value
 3H: How I communicate and create dialog
 4H: The safe spaces and communities for which I gather
 5H: My vital radiance and passion
 6H: Efficiency in my day-to-day operations and service
 7H: My ideal client and influential collaborative relationships
 8H: My capacity to trust in investments and liabilities
 9H: My vision of possibilities and being known to a wide influential audience
10H: My commitment to achieving maximized influential results
11H: My place to be the influencer in bringing together larger platforms and circles
12H: More ease, flow, and restoration to avoid burnout in my brand and business

PERSONALIZE YOUR NEW MOON RITUAL

⬧ What house is being activated? What area of my business is available to add to my intention?

⬧ Do I have any energies/planets within 5° of Leo 16°? If yes, how do those energies want to blend in?

⬧ Do I have any other Fixed energies within 5° of, Taurus, Scorpio, Aquarius 16°? If yes, how do those energies want to add creative friction?

⬧ Do I have any other Fire energies within 5° of Aries or Sagittarius 16°? If yes, how do those energies want to support my new moon intention?

JOURNALING PROMPTS TO DISTILL YOUR INTENTION:

1. Where in your business do you want to show up more confidently?
2. What do you need to believe and feel about yourself to be confident?
3. What do you want to see yourself confidently doing?
4. What in your business brings you the most joy?
5. How can you amplify your joy and spend most of your time doing these things?
6. What does shining brightly in your business mean to you?
7. Where in your brand do you want to influence? Influence who? To accomplish what?
8. What needs to be created in your business with pride and heart? What does that look like for your brand?

_____

_____

_____

_____

_____

_____

_____

_____

_____

_____

Today _____
DATE

I, _____,
NAME

plant the seeds of confidently shining
brighter with heart-centered purpose
in my business:

[[Write your New Moon intention and speak it out loud.
Return to this often.]]

What do I want?

_____

_____

Why do I want this?

_____

_____

How do I want to feel as/when I manifest this?

_____

_____

NEW MOON SEPTEMBER 2021
VIRGO 14°

· ·

 Today I plant the seeds of healthy systems that effectively serve others in my business and brand.

September 7/8, 2021
September 7 5:52 PM PT / 8:52 PM ET
September 8 12:52 AM GMT / 10:52 AM AEST / 12:52 PM NZST

A healthy business is an effective system that works symbiotically for you, the business owner, for those you serve and for those that serve you. You, as the owner of the system get to diagnose and call in help in order for you to help yourself and others.

Whether you are called to bring in more automations so you can do more with less, or you are wont to build a streamlined system to serve many more people, you have the ability to chart the way to make your business whole and healthy.

Remember, you are not meant to do it alone. Delegate effectively. Work effectively.

Decide today what do you want in your business to be more healthy and systemized? Look at what has caused pain and frustration before as to where you need to start.

Cosmic Notes for the Astro Geeks

- ◇ New Moon trine Uranus
- ◇ Mercury opposite Chiron in Aries
- ◇ Pluto trine Mars
- ◇ Jupiter trine Venus

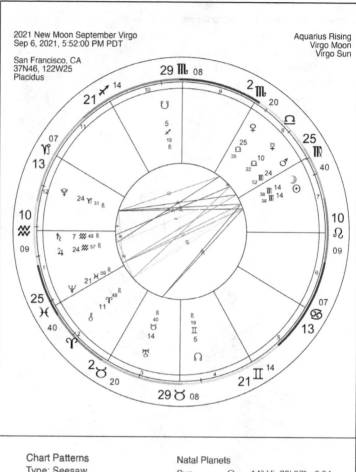

2021 New Moon September Virgo
Sep 6, 2021, 5:52:00 PM PDT

San Francisco, CA
37N46, 122W25
Placidus

Aquarius Rising
Virgo Moon
Virgo Sun

Chart Patterns

Type: Seesaw
Ruler Asc: Uranus

Elements/Modes

Fire	1
Earth	7
Air	6
Water	2

Cardinal	4
Fixed	6
Mutable	6

Strong: Earth, Air

Natal Planets

Sun	☉	14° Vir 38' 07"	6.04
Moon	☽	14° Vir 38' 17"	10.60
Mercury	☿	10° Lib 22'	-5.59
Venus	♀	25° Lib 35'	-10.41
Mars	♂	24° Vir 52'	2.84
Jupiter	♃	24° Aqu 57'R	-14.33
Saturn	♄	7° Aqu 48'R	-19.10
Uranus	♅	14° Tau 40'R	15.83
Neptune	♆	21° Pis 59'R	-4.25
Pluto	♇	24° Cap 31'R	-22.82
Chiron	⚷	11° Ari 48'R	6.87
N Node	☊	5° Gem 19'R	21.18
Asc.	⊖	10° Aqu 09'	
MC	☊	29° Sco 08'	

HOUSE ACTIVATIONS TO PERSONALIZE YOUR NEW MOON RITUAL

Today I plant the seeds to build healthy systems and effectively serve others through my business's:

1H: Health-focused brand identity and leadership style
2H: Holistic values and value add to my customers
3H: Organized and detailed communications and promotions
4H: Integrated safe spaces for emotional groundedness
5H: Joy and pleasure from nature
6H: Effective and daily routines that help others
7H: Organic partnerships with my ideal customers and co-creators
8H: Ability to diagnose, detoxify and heal with nature
9H: Expansion and ideal vision of helping others
10H: Organized, responsibility-driven mission in my work
11H: Social and environmental impact for healthy communities
12H: Elevation above perfectionism to reach empathy for one's highest self

PERSONALIZE YOUR NEW MOON RITUAL

◊ What house is being activated? What area of my business is available to add to my intention?
◊ Do I have any energies/planets within 5° of Virgo 14°? If yes, how do those energies want to blend in?
◊ Do I have any other Mutable energies within 5° of, Gemini, Sagittarius, Pisces 14°? If yes, how do those energies want to add creative friction?
◊ Do I have any other Earth energies within 5° of Taurus or Capricorn 14°? If yes, how do those energies want to support my new moon intention?

JOURNALING PROMPTS TO DISTILL YOUR INTENTION:

1. What does a healthy business look like for you?
2. What in my business needs to be more organized?
3. What do I want in a daily or weekly routine in my business?
4. Where in my business do I need to bring wholeness and wellness? What gaps do I want to fill in?
5. What does effectiveness look like in my business?
6. How do I want to be of service to my clients & my community?

_____

_____

_____

_____

_____

_____

_____

_____

_____

_____

_____

Today _____
DATE

I, _____ ,
NAME

plant the seeds of healthy systems that

effectively serve others in my business:

[[Write your New Moon intention and speak it out loud.
Return to this often.]]

What do I want?

_____

_____

Why do I want this?

_____

_____

How do I want to feel as/when I manifest this?

_____

_____

NEW MOON OCTOBER 2021
LIBRA 13°

· ·

Today I plant the seeds to rethink collaborations and re-call in my soul customers in my business and brand.

October 6/7, 2021
October 6 4:05 AM PT / 7:05 AM ET / 11:05 AM GMT / 9:05 PM AEST
October 7 12:05 AM NZST

Our last Mercury Retrograde in Air for 2021 flavors our Libra New Moon. It's time to rethink partnerships and reorganize your collaborations. What has shifted for you with committing to and calling in your ideal customers, your contractors, or your co-creators?

We rise together is the theme. Yet, what needs revisiting? What has caused pain in partnerships? What new thoughts have come up?

You have great drive and initiative when the partnership is right. Pay attention to your motivation. If excitement is replaced by anxiety or frustration, something requires rethinking.

Decide today what soul customers, partnerships and collaborations you want in your spiritual business. Your individuality serves the partnership, not to compromise in order to make peace.

Cosmic Notes for the Astro Geeks

- ✧ New Moon conjunct Mars, opposite Chiron
- ✧ Mercury retrograde
- ✧ Inconjunct Uranus

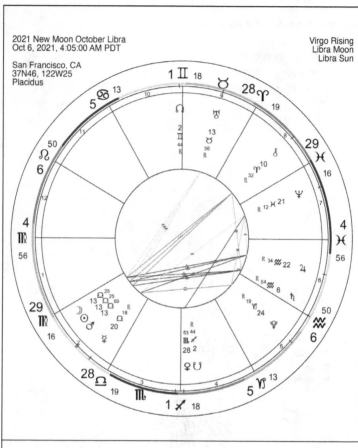

2021 New Moon October Libra
Oct 6, 2021, 4:05:00 AM PDT

San Francisco, CA
37N46, 122W25
Placidus

Virgo Rising
Libra Moon
Libra Sun

Chart Patterns

Type: Funnel
  leading Moon
  focus Uranus
Ruler Asc: Mercury

Elements/Modes

Fire	1
Earth	4
Air	9
Water	2
Cardinal	8
Fixed	4
Mutable	4
Strong: Air	

Natal Planets

Sun	☉	13° Lib 24' 50"	-5.29
Moon	☽	13° Lib 24' 39"	-1.70
Mercury	☿	20° Lib 18'R	-10.52
Venus	♀	28° Sco 53'	-22.39
Mars	♂	13° Lib 59'	-4.89
Jupiter	♃	22° Aqu 34'R	-15.09
Saturn	♄	6° Aqu 54'R	-19.34
Uranus	♅	13° Tau 56'R	15.61
Neptune	♆	21° Pis 12'R	-4.56
Pluto	♇	24° Cap 19'R	-22.88
Chiron	⚷	10° Ari 32'R	6.35
N Node	☊	2° Gem 44'R	20.70
Asc.	Θ	4° Vir 56'	
MC	⊕	1° Gem 18'	

HOUSE ACTIVATIONS TO PERSONALIZE YOUR NEW MOON RITUAL

Today I plant the seeds to partner, cocreate and call in my soul customers through my business's:

- 1H: Friendly and welcoming brand and guidance
- 2H: Kindness-based values and value add to my customers
- 3H: Peaceful communications and promotional messaging
- 4H: Loving, connected, emotional safe spaces
- 5H: Collaborative pleasure, joy, and purposeful creativity
- 6H: Balanced routines and systems
- 7H: Connections with peaceful warrior ideal customers and co-creators
- 8H: Relationship healing and transformation
- 9H: Joint ventures and partnered public relations
- 10H: Delivering in partnership you ultimate mission
- 11H: Alliances for diplomacy and peaceful community building
- 12H: Harmonized and balanced renewal

PERSONALIZE YOUR NEW MOON RITUAL

⬧ What house is being activated? What area of my business is available to add to my intention?

⬧ Do I have any energies/planets within 5° of Libra 13°? If yes, how do those energies want to blend in?

⬧ Do I have any other Cardinal energies within 5° of, Aries, Cancer, Capricorn 13°? If yes, how do those energies want to add creative friction?

⬧ Do I have any other Air energies within 5° of Gemini or Aquarius 13°? If yes, how do those energies want to support my new moon intention?

JOURNALING PROMPTS TO DISTILL YOUR INTENTION

In your business and brand:

1. What do you need to rethink about partnership?
2. Are there existing partnerships that need to be reorganized?
3. What do you want to create in partnership?
4. With whom do you want to co-create?
5. Who do you want to support?
6. What do these partnerships feel like?
7. What is your role and energy in this partnership?
8. What is the result of this partnership?

Today _____
DATE

I, _____ ,
NAME

plant the seeds to rethink collaborations and

re-call in my soul customers in my business:

[[Write your New Moon intention and speak it out loud.
Return to this often.]]

What do I want?

_____

_____

Why do I want this?

_____

_____

How do I want to feel as/when I manifest this?

_____

_____

SUPER NEW MOON NOVEMBER 2021
SCORPIO 12°
· ·

*Today I plant the seeds to trust
my intuition and authentic power
in my business and brand.*

November 4/5, 2021
November 4 2:15 PM PT / 5:15 PM ET / 9:15 PM GMT
November 5 7:15 AM AEST / 10:15 AM NZST

Do you use your intuition in business? Our Intuition is our authentic power and for so many of us, we are out of touch with our intuition as it's been systematically disconnected from the way we run our businesses.

Hearing our intuition takes trust and listening.

How are you listening? Are your trusting? What decisions are you making on intuition vs fear? When intuition communicates, it's neutral, there is not an emotional charge like fear being passed. If you feel fear, can you dive deeper into the fear below the fear where things are calm to access your intuition? This takes Scorpio stillness. Scorpio trust. Trust in oneself. This is our authentic power.

When you can make decisions from this seat of your power, breakthrough and magic happen in your business.

Decide today that you want to trust your intuition and how you want it to guide you in your spiritual business. On your individual intuitive terms.

Cosmic Notes for the Astro Geeks

- ◊ Supermoon - closest distance to the Earth in its orbit
- ◊ Opposite Uranus

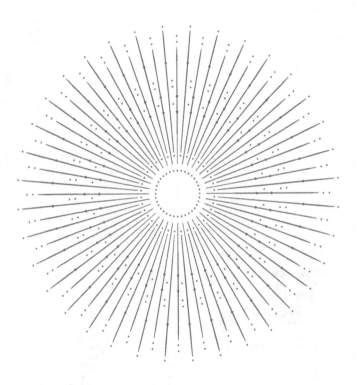

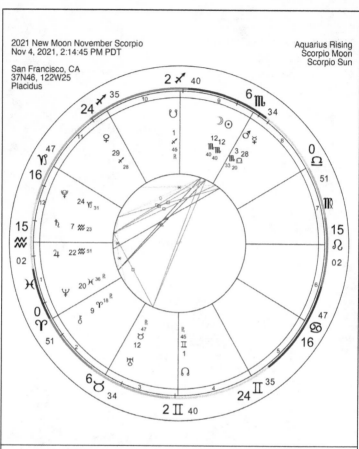

2021 New Moon November Scorpio
Nov 4, 2021, 2:14:45 PM PDT

Aquarius Rising
Scorpio Moon
Scorpio Sun

San Francisco, CA
37N46, 122W25
Placitus

Chart Patterns

Type: Funnel
  leading Mercury
  focus Uranus
Ruler Asc: Uranus
Asp Pat: T-Square
  to Saturn

Elements/Modes

Fire	3
Earth	2
Air	5
Water	6

Cardinal	3
Fixed	10
Mutable	3

Strong: Water

Natal Planets

Sun	☉	12° Sco 40' 13"	-15.63
Moon	☽	12° Sco 40' 20"	-13.99
Mercury	☿	28° Lib 20'	-9.14
Venus	♀	29° Sag 28'	-27.22
Mars	♂	3° Sco 33'	-12.29
Jupiter	♃	22° Aqu 51'	-14.94
Saturn	♄	7° Aqu 23'	-19.21
Uranus	♅	12° Tau 47'R	15.27
Neptune	♆	20° Pis 36'R	-4.79
Pluto	♇	24° Cap 31'	-22.86
Chiron	⚷	9° Ari 18'R	5.82
N Node	☊	1° Gem 45'R	20.50
Asc.	⊖	15° Aqu 02'	
MC	⊕	2° Sag 40'	

HOUSE ACTIVATIONS TO PERSONALIZE YOUR NEW MOON RITUAL

Today I plant the seeds trust my intuition and authentic power in my business's:

- 1H: Personal brand and honest leadership style
- 2H: Faithful values and loyalty to my customers
- 3H: Unapologetic communications and promotional messaging
- 4H: Safe spaces to hold vulnerable emotional security
- 5H: Pleasurable, creative, dramatic, power play
- 6H: Holistic operations that eliminate everything unnecessary
- 7H: Transformative partnerships with ideal customers and co-creators
- 8H: Deeply intuitive and mystical therapeutic abilities
- 9H: Divine knowledge and philosophy
- 10H: Highest visibility and delivery of spiritual truth
- 11H: Community and platform of other truth seekers
- 12H: Profound sense to make peace and surrender

PERSONALIZE YOUR NEW MOON RITUAL

- ◊ What house is being activated? What area of my business is available to add to my intention?
- ◊ Do I have any energies/planets within 5° of Scorpio 12°? If yes, how do those energies want to blend in?
- ◊ Do I have any other Fixed energies within 5° of, Taurus, Leo, Aquarius 12°? If yes, how do those energies want to add creative friction?
- ◊ Do I have any other Water energies within 5° of Cancer or Pisces 12°? If yes, how do those energies want to support my new moon intention?

JOURNALING PROMPTS TO DISTILL YOUR INTENTION

For Super New Moons, think about these questions in three layers:
- ◊ Personal, self, and body
- ◊ Business and community
- ◊ Collective, environmental, Mother Earth

1. What is your authentic power and how does it show up in your business?
2. How do you sense your intuition? How do you want to amplify that sensation?
3. What can you do to trust your intuition and authentic power?
4. How do you want to harness your intuition in your business?
5. How do you want to grow your authentic power in your business?

_____

_____

_____

_____

_____

_____

_____

_____

_____

_____

Today _____
                    DATE

I, _____ ,
                    NAME

plant the seeds to trust my intuition and

authentic power in my business:

[[Write your New Moon intention and speak it out loud.
Return to this often.]]

What do I want?

_____

_____

Why do I want this?

_____

_____

How do I want to feel as/when I manifest this?

_____

_____

SUPER NEW MOON DECEMBER 2021
SAGITTARIUS 12° (SOLAR ECLIPSE)

· ·

*Today I plant the seeds to
expand the horizons of
my business and brand.*

December 3/4, 2021
December 3 11:43 PM PT
December 4 2:43 AM ET / 7:43 AM GMT / 5:43 PM NZST PT
8:34 AM NZST

Woo hoo you made it. Thank you, 2021! Move over for visions for 2022!

With this powerful Solar Eclipse New Moon, let your New Moon intentions be more free flow and less specific as there could be some wild
cards at play.

But you can't let the last New Moon of 2021 go without ado.

This time, pay gratitude and ask for more.

Gratitude is the key to abundance. There is grace in everything, even
the most challenging of circumstances. What are you thankful for?

And next, what do you want MORE of!? Reach more people, grow, expand, vision, purpose, outreach

Decide today that you have an abundance of gratitude for 2021 and
what you want more of in 2022. Your words of gratitude and optimism
have power.

Cosmic Notes for the Astro Geeks

- ◊ Conjunct Mercury
- ◊ Inconjunct Uranus
- ◊ Venus conjunct Pluto

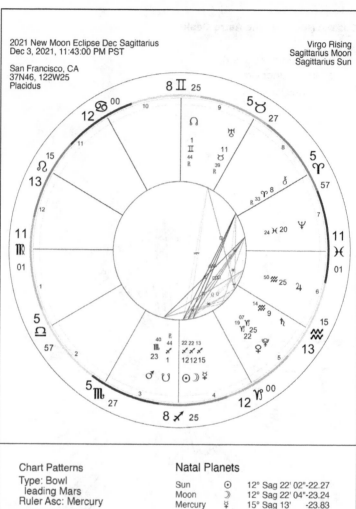

2021 New Moon Eclipse Dec Sagittarius
Dec 3, 2021, 11:43:00 PM PST

Virgo Rising
Sagittarius Moon
Sagittarius Sun

San Francisco, CA
37N46, 122W25
Placidus

Chart Patterns

Type: Bowl
  leading Mars
Ruler Asc: Mercury

Elements/Modes

Fire	6
Earth	5
Air	3
Water	2

Cardinal	3
Fixed	4
Mutable	9

Strong: Fire

Natal Planets

Sun	☉	12° Sag 22' 02"	-22.27
Moon	☽	12° Sag 22' 04"	-23.24
Mercury	☿	15° Sag 13'	-23.83
Venus	♀	22° Cap 19'	-24.16
Mars	♂	23° Sco 40'	-18.53
Jupiter	♃	25° Aqu 50'	-13.88
Saturn	♄	9° Aqu 14'	-18.73
Uranus	♅	11° Tau 39'R	14.93
Neptune	♆	20° Pis 24'	-4.85
Pluto	♇	25° Cap 07'	-22.77
Chiron	⚷	8° Ari 33'R	5.45
N Node	☊	1° Gem 44'R	20.50
Asc.	Θ	11° Vir 01'	
MC	Ⓜ	8° Gem 25'	

HOUSE ACTIVATIONS TO PERSONALIZE YOUR NEW MOON RITUAL

Today I plant the seeds to expand the horizons and reach through my business's:

1H: Brand identity and expanding leadership
2H: Gratitude-based values and value add
3H: Inspirational communications and promotional messaging
4H: Emotional groundedness and deep roots to rise high
5H: Expansive pleasure, joy and creative purpose in all projects
6H: Daily, effect operations, that let you serve many more
7H: Collaboration with cosmopolitan ideal customers and co-creators
8H: Ability to transform and heal using diverse wisdom traditions
9H: Global reach, visibility and ideal vision
10H: Amplified delivery of your ultimate mission on the global stage
11H: International social impact and community building
12H: Journeying for unification with one's highest self

PERSONALIZE YOUR NEW MOON RITUAL

◊ What house is being activated? What area of my business is available to add to my intention?
◊ Do I have any energies/planets within 5° of Sagittarius 12°? If yes, how do those energies want to blend in?
◊ Do I have any other Mutable energies within 5° of, Gemini, Virgo, Pisces 12°? If yes, how do those energies want to add creative friction?
◊ Do I have any other Fire energies within 5° of Aries or Leo 12°? If yes, how do those energies want to support my new moon intention?

For Eclipses, be as general and wide as possible. Wild cards can be thrown.

Part 1: Gratitude:

1. For what are you grateful for?
2. What wonderful things happened this year?
3. What challenging things happened this year and what were the silver linings?

Part 2: What do you want more of in 2022?

1. What parts of your business do you want to grow?
2. What is the reach you want to have with your business in 2022?
3. How do you want your business to expand its visibility?

Today _____
DATE

I, _____ ,
NAME

plant the seeds to expand my horizons

and reach in my business:

[[Write your New Moon intention and speak it out loud.
Return to this often.]]

What do I want?

_____

_____

Why do I want this?

_____

_____

How do I want to feel as/when I manifest this?

_____

_____

CLOSING WORDS

Like our ancestors for millenia, you too can work with Lunar phases in your life and business. Your business is a beautiful garden, with the right tending, nourishing, and working with its seasons, it can blossom in the way you intend.

Practice these New Moon rituals by yourself or with a circle of trusted friends. In circle, the power amplifies, as each individual helps nourish each others' intentions.

There is no wrong or right way to do these rituals. Do what feels good to you.

I hope that you find as much joy and success in your life and business as you create space to work with the power of the Moon.

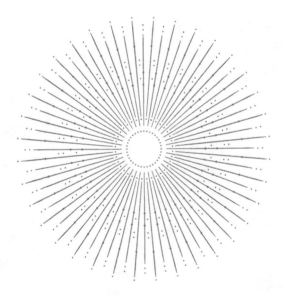

ABOUT THE AUTHOR

I'm Leslie Tagorda (she/her), a multiracial, brand astrologer, and strategist. An Aquarius boss woman and Human Design Projector, I call myself a Brand Navigator as I guide transformational visionaries to reach for and exceed their expectations using my own system of an empowered brand and biz astrology called The AstroBrand Method™.

Since 2004 I've helped hundreds of entrepreneurs and social impact organizations clarify their brand story, express themselves through their websites, social and brands so they can stop hiding and shine brighter like the luminaries they are meant to be.

I host a podcast and Facebook community The Savvy Luminary – Astrology for Entrepreneurs. And when not stargazing and advising, I'm a professional classical clarinetist touring with my nationally-recognized chamber ensemble or playing in the pits of groups like the San Francisco Ballet and the San Francisco Opera.

I currently reside in the occupied land of the Ohlone Ramaytush currently called San Francisco with my husband and son.

- ✧ Listen to my weekly astrology for entrepreneurs podcast on your favorite podcast player: The Savvy Luminary
- ✧ Schedule a breakthrough AstroBrand™ session where we chart your star-powered brand and position it exactly to your design (leadership role, true values, ideal customer astrographics (archetype + psychographics), brand visibility and communication style- I can see all of this in your chart)
  Newmooncreative.co/astrobrand

🎧 Podcast: TheSavvyLuminary.com
📷 Instagram: @newmooncreativeco
f Facebook Group: facebook.com/groups/TheSavvyLuminary
▶ Youtube: youtube.com/c/NewMoonCreativeCo

CPSIA information can be obtained
at www.ICGtesting.com
Printed in the USA
FSHW010729081220